Glucose Revolution Cookbook

*Recipes and Tips for Balancing Blood
Sugar, Inspired by Jessie Inchauspé*

Angela W. Hill

Copyright © 2024

All rights reserved. No part of this publication may be reproduced, distributed, or transmitted in any form or by any means, including photocopying, recording, or other electronic or mechanical methods, without the prior written permission of the publisher, except in the case of brief quotations embodied in critical reviews and certain other non-commercial uses permitted by copyright law.

Table of Contents

Introduction
Chapter 1: Setting the Stage for a New Way of Eating
    Food as Fuel: Why What You Eat Matters
    Key Principles for Success in the Kitchen
    Setting Up Your Kitchen for Success
    What's Next?
Chapter 2: Energizing Breakfast Recipes
    Egg Muffins with Spinach and Peppers
    Quinoa Breakfast Bowl with Berries
    Avocado and Cottage Cheese Bowl
    Cauliflower Rice Breakfast Bowl
    Smoked Salmon and Avocado Toast
    Coconut Chia Seed Pudding
    Spinach and Feta Omelet
    Zucchini Fritters
    Smoked Turkey and Veggie Scramble
    Scrambled Tofu with Vegetables
Chapter 3: Hearty Lunch Recipes
    Chicken and Avocado Salad
    Zucchini Noodles with Pesto and Shrimp
    Greek Quinoa Salad
    Grilled Salmon with Asparagus
    Stuffed Bell Peppers with Turkey and Spinach
    Chicken Lettuce Wraps
    Spaghetti Squash with Marinara and Ground Beef
    Cobb Salad
    Broccoli and Cheddar Soup

- Grilled Chicken Caesar Salad

Chapter 4: Light Dinners to End the Day Right
- Lemon Garlic Baked Salmon with Broccoli
- Zucchini Noodles with Ground Turkey and Tomato Sauce
- Grilled Chicken and Avocado Salad
- Baked Cod with Lemon and Asparagus
- Stuffed Bell Peppers with Cauliflower Rice
- Shrimp Stir-Fry with Vegetables
- Eggplant Lasagna
- Cauliflower Fried Rice
- Grilled Steak with Roasted Brussels Sprouts
- Turkey Meatballs with Zucchini Noodles

Chapter 5: Guilt-Free Snacks and Sides
- Crispy Roasted Chickpeas
- Avocado Deviled Eggs
- Cucumber and Hummus Bites
- Zucchini Chips
- Roasted Brussels Sprouts with Balsamic Glaze
- Almond Butter Energy Bites
- Cauliflower Tots
- Baked Kale Chips
- Stuffed Mini Bell Peppers
- Crispy Parmesan Cauliflower Bites

Chapter 6: Refreshing Drinks and Smoothies
- Green Detox Smoothie
- Coconut Water and Berry Refresher
- Mint and Cucumber Infused Water
- Strawberry Basil Lemonade

- Turmeric Golden Milk
- Lemon Ginger Iced Tea
- Avocado Smoothie
- Cucumber Lemonade
- Kale and Pineapple Smoothie
- Herbal Iced Green Tea

Chapter 7: Sweet Treats Without the Sugar
- Coconut Flour Brownies
- Chia Pudding with Berries
- Almond Butter Chocolate Bites
- Avocado Chocolate Mousse
- Coconut Macaroons
- Baked Apples with Cinnamon
- Lemon Coconut Energy Balls
- Dark Chocolate and Almond Bark
- Berry Parfait with Greek Yogurt
- Peanut Butter and Banana Ice Cream

Bonus: 28-Day Meal Plan for Balanced Glucose
Bonus: 28-Day Meal Plan Shopping List
Bonus: Tips for Long-Term Success
Conclusion

Introduction

Welcome to this cookbook! I'm Angela W. Hill, and I'm thrilled to have you here as we embark on a journey to create delicious, nourishing meals that make you feel great from the inside out. This book is all about finding joy in the kitchen while embracing a way of eating that supports your energy and well-being.

I've always been passionate about food and its power to nourish not just our bodies but also our spirits. Over the years, I've learned how important it is to pay attention to what we eat—not just for our waistlines, but for our overall health and happiness. Through trial and error, I've found that it's possible to enjoy vibrant, flavorful meals that are both satisfying and good for you.

In these pages, you'll find recipes that are designed to make you feel good, both physically and emotionally. Each one is crafted with simple, wholesome ingredients, offering a balance of flavors and textures that you'll love preparing and sharing with others. Whether you're cooking for yourself, your family, or your friends, I've made sure these recipes are approachable, easy to follow, and packed with flavor.

What I hope to show you is that healthy eating doesn't have to be complicated or restrictive. It's about finding the right balance of ingredients that taste great and make you feel even better. You'll discover meals that are comforting, delicious, and nourishing, designed to fuel your day with energy and leave you feeling satisfied.

This book isn't just a collection of recipes—it's an invitation to explore the joy of cooking, to experiment with new flavors, and to discover how the right foods can help you thrive. I'm excited to share these recipes with you, and I hope they bring as much joy to your kitchen as they have to mine.

So, grab your apron, and let's get cooking! I can't wait for you to dive in and start creating meals that not only taste great but also make you feel your best. Together, we'll explore a world of flavors, all while nourishing your body and soul.

Chapter 1: Setting the Stage for a New Way of Eating

Welcome to Chapter 1 of your culinary journey. I'm Angela W. Hill, and before we dive into the recipes that will fill your kitchen with delicious aromas, I want to take a moment to set the stage. In this chapter, we'll explore some essential ideas that will help guide you as you cook your way through this book. Think of it as a blueprint for understanding how to get the most out of these recipes while supporting your overall well-being.

Let me start by sharing a bit of my story. Like many of you, I've spent years trying to find a way of eating that leaves me feeling energized, nourished, and satisfied without constantly chasing the next meal or snack. After plenty of trial and error, I've learned a few key principles that have transformed the way I cook and eat. These are the same principles I've woven into every recipe in this book, and they'll help you discover that healthy eating can be simple, satisfying, and full of flavor.

Food as Fuel: Why What You Eat Matters

We all know that food is fuel, but not all fuel works the same way. The choices we make about what we eat can have a profound impact on how we feel throughout the day. The goal of this book is to help you create meals that not only taste great but also provide you with steady, long-lasting energy.

Think about how you feel after eating a meal that's loaded with refined sugars and empty calories. You might get a quick burst of energy, but it's usually followed by a slump—leaving you tired, sluggish, and looking for your next fix. The recipes in this book are designed to avoid that. Instead, they focus on ingredients that provide nourishment and support balanced energy levels throughout the day.

I've learned that the key to eating well is not deprivation. It's about making choices that support your body and give you the nutrients you need to thrive. You'll find that the recipes in this book feature simple, whole ingredients that are naturally flavorful and satisfying.

Key Principles for Success in the Kitchen

To help you get the most out of this cookbook, I want to introduce a few key principles that will guide you as you prepare these recipes. These aren't strict rules, but rather helpful guidelines that I've found make a world of difference in how I feel after each meal.

1. **Choose Whole Ingredients**: Whenever possible, opt for ingredients that are as close to their natural state as possible. Whole foods are packed with nutrients, fiber, and flavor. The recipes in this book focus on using fresh vegetables, lean proteins, healthy fats, and natural sweeteners that support your body's needs.

2. **Embrace Healthy Fats**: Don't shy away from fats! Healthy fats, like those found in olive oil, nuts, seeds, and avocados, play an essential role in supporting overall health and keeping you satisfied after meals. You'll see these ingredients used generously throughout the book because they help to slow digestion and provide steady energy.
3. **Focus on Balance**: Each recipe is designed with balance in mind. You'll notice that the meals combine healthy fats, proteins, and fiber-rich ingredients that work together to support your well-being. By creating a balance on your plate, you'll feel full and energized without the need for constant snacking.
4. **Be Mindful of Portions**: While the recipes are all designed to nourish and satisfy, it's still important to be mindful of portion sizes. Eating slowly and savoring your meal helps you tune into your body's signals, so you know when you're full.
5. **Enjoy the Process**: Cooking should be enjoyable! This book isn't about strict rules or rigid guidelines. It's about discovering the joy of preparing meals that make you feel good. Take your time, experiment with flavors, and don't be afraid to make these recipes your own.

Setting Up Your Kitchen for Success

To help you get started on the right foot, it's worth taking a moment to think about how you set up your kitchen. Having the right ingredients on hand can make a huge difference when it comes to sticking with a new way of cooking. Here are a few pantry staples that will make preparing these recipes easier and more convenient:

- **Olive oil**: A healthy fat that's perfect for cooking and drizzling over salads.
- **Nuts and seeds**: Great for adding texture and flavor to dishes, as well as providing healthy fats and protein.
- **Fresh vegetables**: Stock up on greens, root vegetables, and other seasonal produce to build nutrient-dense meals.
- **Natural sweeteners**: Ingredients like **honey** and **agave** are used in place of refined sugars to provide a touch of sweetness without the crash.
- **Lean proteins**: Chicken, fish, eggs, and plant-based proteins are the foundation of many of the recipes.

By keeping these ingredients on hand, you'll find it easier to whip up a meal that aligns with the principles of balanced, nourishing eating.

What's Next?

Now that you have a solid foundation, it's time to start cooking! In the next chapter, we'll dive into the recipes, beginning with breakfast options that will set you up for success each day. Whether you're a morning person or someone who needs a little extra motivation to start the day, you'll find something here that's both easy to make and deeply satisfying.

I'm so excited to share these recipes with you and help you discover that healthy eating can be both delicious and effortless. As you move through this book, remember that food is meant to be enjoyed. Take your time, savor the process, and feel confident that you're making choices that will leave you feeling your best.

Let's get cooking!

This chapter serves as the foundation for your readers, preparing them to make the most of the recipes that follow while fostering an approachable, enjoyable relationship with food.

Chapter 2: Energizing Breakfast Recipes

Here are 10 breakfast recipes that focus on healthy, nutrient-dense ingredients to provide balanced energy and stable blood sugar throughout the day.

Egg Muffins with Spinach and Peppers

Ingredients:

- 6 large eggs
- 1/2 cup chopped bell peppers
- 1/2 cup chopped spinach
- 1/4 cup shredded cheese (optional)
- Salt and pepper to taste
- 1 tablespoon olive oil

Preparation:

1. Preheat the oven to 350°F (175°C).
2. Grease a muffin tin with olive oil.
3. Whisk the eggs in a bowl and stir in bell peppers, spinach, cheese, salt, and pepper.
4. Pour the egg mixture evenly into the muffin tin cups.
5. Bake for 20 minutes or until the muffins are set and golden.
6. Let cool slightly before serving.

Time: 25 minutes
Nutritional Value (per muffin):
Calories: 120, Protein: 9g, Fat: 8g, Carbs: 2g

Quinoa Breakfast Bowl with Berries

Ingredients:

- 1/2 cup cooked quinoa
- 1/4 cup almond milk
- 1/4 cup mixed berries (blueberries, raspberries, strawberries)
- 1 tablespoon sliced almonds
- 1 tablespoon chia seeds
- 1 teaspoon honey

Preparation:

1. In a bowl, mix the cooked quinoa with almond milk.
2. Top with mixed berries, sliced almonds, and chia seeds.
3. Drizzle with honey and serve.

Time: 10 minutes
Nutritional Value (per serving):
Calories: 310, Protein: 9g, Fat: 12g, Carbs: 42g, Fiber: 9g

Avocado and Cottage Cheese Bowl

Ingredients:

- 1 ripe avocado, diced
- 1/2 cup cottage cheese
- 1 tablespoon olive oil
- 1 tablespoon chopped fresh herbs (such as parsley or cilantro)
- Salt and pepper to taste

Preparation:

1. Place the diced avocado in a bowl.
2. Add cottage cheese and drizzle with olive oil.
3. Sprinkle with fresh herbs, salt, and pepper to taste.
4. Mix gently and serve.

Time: 5 minutes
Nutritional Value (per serving):
Calories: 240, Protein: 10g, Fat: 19g, Carbs: 7g

Cauliflower Rice Breakfast Bowl

Ingredients:

- 1 cup cauliflower rice
- 1 egg
- 1/4 cup diced avocado
- 1/4 cup diced tomatoes
- 1 tablespoon olive oil
- Salt and pepper to taste

Preparation:

1. Heat olive oil in a pan over medium heat.
2. Sauté cauliflower rice until tender, about 5 minutes.
3. In a separate pan, fry the egg until cooked to your liking.
4. Assemble cauliflower rice, avocado, and tomatoes in a bowl.
5. Place the fried egg on top, season with salt and pepper, and serve.

Time: 10 minutes
Nutritional Value (per serving):
Calories: 200, Protein: 8g, Fat: 16g, Carbs: 7g

Smoked Salmon and Avocado Toast

Ingredients:

- 2 slices low-carb or keto-friendly bread
- 2 oz smoked salmon
- 1/2 ripe avocado, mashed
- 1 tablespoon olive oil
- Salt and pepper to taste
- A squeeze of lemon juice

Preparation:

1. Toast the bread.
2. Spread mashed avocado evenly on each slice.
3. Top with smoked salmon and drizzle with olive oil and lemon juice.
4. Season with salt and pepper, and serve immediately.

Time: 10 minutes
Nutritional Value (per serving):
Calories: 300, Protein: 12g, Fat: 22g, Carbs: 10g

Coconut Chia Seed Pudding

Ingredients:

- 1/4 cup chia seeds
- 1 cup unsweetened coconut milk
- 1 tablespoon honey
- 1 teaspoon vanilla extract

Preparation:

1. In a bowl, mix chia seeds, coconut milk, honey, and vanilla extract.
2. Stir well and refrigerate overnight to thicken.
3. Serve chilled with optional toppings like berries or nuts.

Time: 10 minutes prep + overnight setting
Nutritional Value (per serving):
Calories: 230, Protein: 4g, Fat: 15g, Carbs: 17g

Spinach and Feta Omelet

Ingredients:

- 3 large eggs
- 1/4 cup crumbled feta cheese
- 1 cup fresh spinach
- 1 tablespoon olive oil
- Salt and pepper to taste

Preparation:

1. Heat olive oil in a pan over medium heat.
2. Sauté the spinach until wilted, about 2 minutes.
3. In a bowl, whisk the eggs and season with salt and pepper.
4. Pour the eggs over the spinach and cook until almost set.
5. Sprinkle feta cheese on top, fold the omelet, and serve hot.

Time: 10 minutes
Nutritional Value (per serving):
Calories: 270, Protein: 18g, Fat: 21g, Carbs: 3g

Zucchini Fritters

Ingredients:

- 2 zucchinis, grated
- 1/4 cup almond flour
- 1 egg
- 2 tablespoons olive oil
- Salt and pepper to taste

Preparation:

1. Squeeze excess water from the grated zucchini.
2. In a bowl, mix zucchini, almond flour, and egg.
3. Heat olive oil in a pan over medium heat.
4. Drop spoonfuls of the mixture into the pan, flattening into fritters.
5. Fry for 3-4 minutes on each side until golden brown.
6. Serve warm.

Time: 20 minutes
Nutritional Value (per fritter):
Calories: 150, Protein: 5g, Fat: 12g, Carbs: 5g

Smoked Turkey and Veggie Scramble

Ingredients:

- 3 large eggs
- 1/4 cup diced smoked turkey
- 1/4 cup diced bell pepper
- 1/4 cup chopped spinach
- 1 tablespoon olive oil
- Salt and pepper to taste

Preparation:

1. Heat olive oil in a pan over medium heat.
2. Add bell pepper and smoked turkey, cooking until peppers soften.
3. Stir in spinach and cook until wilted.
4. In a bowl, whisk the eggs and pour into the pan, stirring to scramble.
5. Cook until eggs are set, then season with salt and pepper.

Time: 15 minutes
Nutritional Value (per serving):
Calories: 230, Protein: 20g, Fat: 16g, Carbs: 4g

Scrambled Tofu with Vegetables

Ingredients:

- 1/2 block firm tofu, crumbled
- 1/2 cup chopped spinach
- 1/4 cup diced tomatoes
- 1/4 teaspoon turmeric
- 1 tablespoon olive oil
- Salt and pepper to taste

Preparation:

1. Heat olive oil in a pan over medium heat.
2. Add crumbled tofu and turmeric, stirring until tofu is heated.
3. Stir in spinach and tomatoes, cooking until spinach wilts.
4. Season with salt and pepper, then serve.

Time: 10 minutes
Nutritional Value (per serving):
Calories: 180, Protein: 10g, Fat: 12g, Carbs: 5g

These breakfast recipes offer a variety of flavors and ingredients, all tailored to provide you with balanced, nourishing meals to fuel your day.

Chapter 3: Hearty Lunch Recipes

After a balanced and energizing breakfast, the next important step is a satisfying, nutrient-dense lunch that will sustain you through the rest of the day. In this chapter, you'll find ten delicious lunch recipes that focus on clean, whole ingredients to keep your glucose levels steady and your energy high.

Chicken and Avocado Salad

Ingredients:

- 2 cups mixed greens
- 1 cooked chicken breast, sliced
- 1 ripe avocado, diced
- 1/2 cup cherry tomatoes, halved
- 1 tablespoon olive oil
- 1 tablespoon lemon juice
- Salt and pepper to taste

Preparation:

1. In a large bowl, toss mixed greens with chicken, avocado, and cherry tomatoes.
2. Drizzle with olive oil and lemon juice.
3. Season with salt and pepper, then toss to combine.

Time: 10 minutes
Nutritional Value (per serving):
Calories: 350, Protein: 25g, Fat: 25g, Carbs: 8g

Zucchini Noodles with Pesto and Shrimp

Ingredients:

- 2 medium zucchinis, spiralized into noodles
- 1/2 pound shrimp, peeled and deveined
- 2 tablespoons pesto (homemade or store-bought)
- 1 tablespoon olive oil
- Salt and pepper to taste

Preparation:

1. Heat olive oil in a pan over medium heat and cook the shrimp until pink and opaque, about 3 minutes per side.
2. Add zucchini noodles to the pan and cook for 2-3 minutes until slightly softened.
3. Toss with pesto and season with salt and pepper. Serve immediately.

Time: 15 minutes
Nutritional Value (per serving):
Calories: 290, Protein: 25g, Fat: 18g, Carbs: 8g

Greek Quinoa Salad

Ingredients:

- 1 cup cooked quinoa
- 1/2 cup diced cucumber
- 1/2 cup cherry tomatoes, halved
- 1/4 cup crumbled feta cheese
- 1/4 cup Kalamata olives, pitted and halved
- 1 tablespoon olive oil
- 1 tablespoon lemon juice
- 1 teaspoon dried oregano

Preparation:

1. In a bowl, combine cooked quinoa, cucumber, tomatoes, feta cheese, and olives.
2. Drizzle with olive oil and lemon juice.
3. Sprinkle with oregano and toss to combine.

Time: 10 minutes
Nutritional Value (per serving):
Calories: 310, Protein: 10g, Fat: 14g, Carbs: 35g

Grilled Salmon with Asparagus

Ingredients:

- 1 salmon fillet
- 1 tablespoon olive oil
- 1 clove garlic, minced
- 1 bunch asparagus, trimmed
- Salt and pepper to taste
- Lemon wedges for serving

Preparation:

1. Preheat grill or grill pan to medium-high heat.
2. Drizzle salmon and asparagus with olive oil, and season with garlic, salt, and pepper.
3. Grill salmon for 4-5 minutes per side until cooked through. Grill asparagus for 3-4 minutes until tender.
4. Serve with lemon wedges.

Time: 15 minutes
Nutritional Value (per serving):
Calories: 350, Protein: 30g, Fat: 24g, Carbs: 6g

Stuffed Bell Peppers with Turkey and Spinach

Ingredients:

- 4 bell peppers, tops cut off and seeds removed
- 1 pound ground turkey
- 2 cups spinach, chopped
- 1/2 cup diced tomatoes

- 1 tablespoon olive oil
- Salt and pepper to taste

Preparation:

1. Preheat oven to 375°F (190°C).
2. In a pan, heat olive oil and cook ground turkey until browned.
3. Add spinach and tomatoes, cooking until the spinach wilts.
4. Stuff the bell peppers with the turkey mixture and place in a baking dish.
5. Bake for 25 minutes until peppers are tender.

Time: 40 minutes
Nutritional Value (per serving):
Calories: 280, Protein: 25g, Fat: 12g, Carbs: 10g

Chicken Lettuce Wraps

Ingredients:

- 1 pound ground chicken
- 1 tablespoon olive oil
- 2 tablespoons soy sauce (or tamari for gluten-free)
- 1 tablespoon rice vinegar
- 1/4 cup shredded carrots
- 1/4 cup chopped green onions
- Butter lettuce leaves for wrapping

Preparation:

1. Heat olive oil in a pan and cook ground chicken until browned.
2. Stir in soy sauce, rice vinegar, carrots, and green onions. Cook for 2 minutes.
3. Serve in lettuce leaves as wraps.

Time: 15 minutes
Nutritional Value (per serving):
Calories: 250, Protein: 24g, Fat: 14g, Carbs: 6g

Spaghetti Squash with Marinara and Ground Beef

Ingredients:

- 1 medium spaghetti squash
- 1/2 pound ground beef
- 1 cup marinara sauce (low sugar)
- 1 tablespoon olive oil
- Salt and pepper to taste

Preparation:

1. Preheat oven to 400°F (200°C). Cut the spaghetti squash in half, remove seeds, and roast cut side down for 30-40 minutes.
2. Meanwhile, heat olive oil in a pan and cook ground beef until browned.
3. Stir in marinara sauce and simmer for 5 minutes.
4. Scrape the spaghetti squash into strands and top with the beef marinara mixture.

Time: 45 minutes
Nutritional Value (per serving):
Calories: 320, Protein: 20g, Fat: 18g, Carbs: 14g

Cobb Salad

Ingredients:

- 2 cups mixed greens
- 1 cooked chicken breast, diced
- 2 hard-boiled eggs, sliced
- 1/2 avocado, diced
- 1/4 cup crumbled blue cheese
- 2 slices cooked bacon, crumbled
- 1 tablespoon olive oil
- 1 tablespoon red wine vinegar
- Salt and pepper to taste

Preparation:

1. In a large bowl, arrange the greens, chicken, eggs, avocado, blue cheese, and bacon.
2. Drizzle with olive oil and vinegar.
3. Season with salt and pepper, then toss to combine.

Time: 10 minutes
Nutritional Value (per serving):
Calories: 450, Protein: 32g, Fat: 34g, Carbs: 8g

Broccoli and Cheddar Soup

Ingredients:

- 2 cups broccoli florets
- 1/2 cup shredded cheddar cheese
- 1 cup unsweetened almond milk
- 1/2 cup chicken broth
- 1 tablespoon olive oil
- 1 clove garlic, minced
- Salt and pepper to taste

Preparation:

1. Heat olive oil in a pan and sauté garlic until fragrant.
2. Add broccoli and cook for 5 minutes.
3. Stir in almond milk and chicken broth, simmer for 10 minutes until broccoli is tender.
4. Blend the soup until smooth, then stir in cheddar cheese until melted. Season with salt and pepper.

Time: 20 minutes
Nutritional Value (per serving):
Calories: 250, Protein: 12g, Fat: 18g, Carbs: 10g

Grilled Chicken Caesar Salad

Ingredients:

- 1 grilled chicken breast, sliced
- 2 cups romaine lettuce
- 1/4 cup grated Parmesan cheese
- 2 tablespoons Caesar dressing (low-carb)
- 1 tablespoon olive oil
- Salt and pepper to taste

Preparation:

1. In a large bowl, toss romaine lettuce with Parmesan cheese, olive oil, and Caesar dressing.
2. Top with grilled chicken slices.
3. Season with salt and pepper, and serve.

Time: 10 minutes
Nutritional Value (per serving):
Calories: 320, Protein: 28g, Fat: 22g, Carbs: 6g

These hearty lunch recipes are packed with nutrients, low in carbs, and designed to keep your glucose levels balanced while keeping you satisfied throughout the day

Chapter 4: Light Dinners to End the Day Right

Dinner is an important meal where you want to feel satisfied but not overly full. This chapter will provide 10 light yet satisfying dinner recipes that help you wind down your day with balanced nutrition, ensuring steady glucose levels while keeping the flavors vibrant and fulfilling.

Lemon Garlic Baked Salmon with Broccoli

Ingredients:

- 1 salmon fillet
- 1 tablespoon olive oil
- 1 clove garlic, minced
- Juice of 1 lemon
- 1 cup broccoli florets
- Salt and pepper to taste

Preparation:

1. Preheat the oven to 375°F (190°C).
2. Place the salmon and broccoli on a baking sheet, drizzle with olive oil, lemon juice, and garlic, and season with salt and pepper.
3. Bake for 15-20 minutes, until the salmon is cooked through and the broccoli is tender.

Time: 20 minutes
Nutritional Value (per serving):
Calories: 320, Protein: 30g, Fat: 18g, Carbs: 8g

Zucchini Noodles with Ground Turkey and Tomato Sauce

Ingredients:

- 2 zucchinis, spiralized into noodles
- 1/2 pound ground turkey
- 1 cup tomato sauce (low-sugar)
- 1 tablespoon olive oil
- Salt and pepper to taste

Preparation:

1. Heat olive oil in a pan and cook the ground turkey until browned.
2. Add tomato sauce and simmer for 5 minutes.
3. Sauté the zucchini noodles in a separate pan for 2-3 minutes, until tender.
4. Serve the turkey sauce over the zucchini noodles.

Time: 15 minutes
Nutritional Value (per serving):
Calories: 270, Protein: 24g, Fat: 15g, Carbs: 10g

Grilled Chicken and Avocado Salad

Ingredients:

- 1 grilled chicken breast, sliced
- 2 cups mixed greens
- 1 ripe avocado, diced
- 1/4 cup cherry tomatoes, halved
- 1 tablespoon olive oil
- 1 tablespoon balsamic vinegar
- Salt and pepper to taste

Preparation:

1. In a large bowl, combine mixed greens, avocado, cherry tomatoes, and grilled chicken.
2. Drizzle with olive oil and balsamic vinegar, and toss.
3. Season with salt and pepper, and serve.

Time: 10 minutes
Nutritional Value (per serving):
Calories: 350, Protein: 30g, Fat: 24g, Carbs: 8g

Baked Cod with Lemon and Asparagus

Ingredients:

- 1 cod fillet
- 1 tablespoon olive oil
- Juice of 1 lemon
- 1 bunch asparagus, trimmed
- Salt and pepper to taste

Preparation:

1. Preheat oven to 375°F (190°C).
2. Place the cod and asparagus on a baking sheet, drizzle with olive oil and lemon juice, and season with salt and pepper.
3. Bake for 15-20 minutes, until the cod is flaky and the asparagus is tender.

Time: 20 minutes
Nutritional Value (per serving):
Calories: 280, Protein: 28g, Fat: 12g, Carbs: 6g

Stuffed Bell Peppers with Cauliflower Rice

Ingredients:

- 4 bell peppers, tops cut off and seeds removed
- 1 cup cauliflower rice
- 1/2 pound ground beef
- 1/4 cup diced onions
- 1 tablespoon olive oil
- 1 cup tomato sauce (low-sugar)
- Salt and pepper to taste

Preparation:

1. Preheat oven to 375°F (190°C).
2. Heat olive oil in a pan, cook ground beef and onions until browned, then stir in cauliflower rice and tomato sauce.
3. Stuff the bell peppers with the beef mixture and place them in a baking dish.
4. Bake for 30 minutes, until the peppers are tender.

Time: 40 minutes
Nutritional Value (per serving):
Calories: 310, Protein: 22g, Fat: 15g, Carbs: 10g

Shrimp Stir-Fry with Vegetables

Ingredients:

- 1/2 pound shrimp, peeled and deveined
- 1 cup broccoli florets
- 1/2 cup bell peppers, sliced
- 1 tablespoon soy sauce (or tamari for gluten-free)
- 1 tablespoon olive oil
- Salt and pepper to taste

Preparation:

1. Heat olive oil in a pan and cook shrimp until pink, about 2-3 minutes per side.
2. Add broccoli and bell peppers, stir-fry until tender.
3. Stir in soy sauce and cook for another 2 minutes. Serve hot.

Time: 15 minutes
Nutritional Value (per serving):
Calories: 240, Protein: 25g, Fat: 12g, Carbs: 8g

Eggplant Lasagna

Ingredients:

- 1 large eggplant, sliced into thin rounds
- 1/2 pound ground turkey
- 1 cup tomato sauce (low-sugar)
- 1/2 cup ricotta cheese
- 1/4 cup mozzarella cheese
- 1 tablespoon olive oil
- Salt and pepper to taste

Preparation:

1. Preheat oven to 375°F (190°C).
2. Heat olive oil in a pan and cook ground turkey until browned, then stir in tomato sauce.
3. Layer the eggplant slices, turkey sauce, ricotta, and mozzarella in a baking dish.
4. Bake for 25-30 minutes, until the eggplant is tender and the cheese is melted.

Time: 40 minutes
Nutritional Value (per serving):
Calories: 350, Protein: 28g, Fat: 20g, Carbs: 10g

Cauliflower Fried Rice

Ingredients:

- 2 cups cauliflower rice
- 1/2 cup diced carrots
- 1/2 cup peas
- 1 egg, lightly beaten
- 1 tablespoon soy sauce (or tamari for gluten-free)
- 1 tablespoon olive oil
- Salt and pepper to taste

Preparation:

1. Heat olive oil in a pan and cook cauliflower rice, carrots, and peas until tender.
2. Push the vegetables to one side of the pan, and pour the beaten egg on the other side, scrambling until cooked.
3. Stir in soy sauce and mix everything together. Serve hot.

Time: 15 minutes
Nutritional Value (per serving):
Calories: 220, Protein: 8g, Fat: 10g, Carbs: 18g

Grilled Steak with Roasted Brussels Sprouts

Ingredients:

- 1 steak (sirloin or ribeye)
- 2 cups Brussels sprouts, halved
- 1 tablespoon olive oil
- Salt and pepper to taste
- 1 clove garlic, minced

Preparation:

1. Preheat oven to 400°F (200°C).
2. Toss Brussels sprouts with olive oil, garlic, salt, and pepper, then roast for 20-25 minutes.
3. Grill the steak over medium heat for 4-5 minutes per side, depending on your preferred doneness.
4. Serve the steak with roasted Brussels sprouts.

Time: 30 minutes
Nutritional Value (per serving):
Calories: 420, Protein: 35g, Fat: 28g, Carbs: 10g

Turkey Meatballs with Zucchini Noodles

Ingredients:

- 1/2 pound ground turkey
- 1 egg
- 1/4 cup almond flour
- 2 zucchinis, spiralized into noodles
- 1 tablespoon olive oil
- 1 cup tomato sauce (low-sugar)
- Salt and pepper to taste

Preparation:

1. Preheat oven to 375°F (190°C).
2. In a bowl, mix ground turkey, egg, almond flour, salt, and pepper. Form into meatballs and bake for 20 minutes.
3. Sauté zucchini noodles in olive oil for 2-3 minutes.
4. Serve meatballs over zucchini noodles, topped with tomato sauce.

Time: 30 minutes
Nutritional Value (per serving):
Calories: 310, Protein: 26g, Fat: 18g, Carbs: 10g

These light but flavorful dinner recipes are designed to keep your glucose levels steady while offering satisfying, nutrient-rich meals.

Chapter 5: Guilt-Free Snacks and Sides

Snacks and side dishes can be tricky when you're trying to maintain balanced glucose levels, but they don't have to be! In this chapter, you'll find 10 quick and delicious snack and side recipes that keep you satisfied while avoiding blood sugar spikes. These are perfect to pair with meals or enjoy between them.

Crispy Roasted Chickpeas

Ingredients:

- 1 can chickpeas, drained and rinsed
- 1 tablespoon olive oil
- 1/2 teaspoon smoked paprika
- 1/2 teaspoon garlic powder
- Salt and pepper to taste

Preparation:

1. Preheat oven to 400°F (200°C).
2. Toss chickpeas with olive oil, paprika, garlic powder, salt, and pepper.
3. Spread evenly on a baking sheet and roast for 25-30 minutes, shaking the pan halfway through for even crisping.

Time: 30 minutes
Nutritional Value (per serving):
Calories: 150, Protein: 7g, Fat: 5g, Carbs: 19g

Avocado Deviled Eggs

Ingredients:

- 6 hard-boiled eggs
- 1 ripe avocado
- 1 tablespoon lime juice
- 1 teaspoon Dijon mustard
- Salt and pepper to taste
- Paprika for garnish (optional)

Preparation:

1. Halve the hard-boiled eggs and scoop out the yolks.
2. Mash the yolks with the avocado, lime juice, Dijon mustard, salt, and pepper.
3. Spoon the mixture back into the egg whites and sprinkle with paprika.

Time: 15 minutes
Nutritional Value (per serving):
Calories: 120, Protein: 6g, Fat: 9g, Carbs: 3g

Cucumber and Hummus Bites

Ingredients:

- 1 cucumber, sliced into rounds
- 1/2 cup hummus (store-bought or homemade)
- 1 tablespoon chopped fresh parsley (optional)

Preparation:

1. Spread a dollop of hummus on each cucumber slice.
2. Garnish with fresh parsley if desired.

Time: 5 minutes
Nutritional Value (per serving):
Calories: 80, Protein: 3g, Fat: 5g, Carbs: 8g

Zucchini Chips

Ingredients:

- 2 zucchinis, thinly sliced
- 1 tablespoon olive oil
- Salt and pepper to taste

Preparation:

1. Preheat oven to 225°F (110°C).
2. Toss zucchini slices with olive oil, salt, and pepper.
3. Arrange slices on a baking sheet and bake for 1.5 to 2 hours, flipping halfway through, until crispy.

Time: 2 hours
Nutritional Value (per serving):
Calories: 50, Protein: 1g, Fat: 4g, Carbs: 5g

Roasted Brussels Sprouts with Balsamic Glaze

Ingredients:

- 2 cups Brussels sprouts, halved
- 1 tablespoon olive oil
- 1 tablespoon balsamic vinegar
- Salt and pepper to taste

Preparation:

1. Preheat oven to 400°F (200°C).
2. Toss Brussels sprouts with olive oil, balsamic vinegar, salt, and pepper.
3. Roast for 20-25 minutes, until golden and crispy.

Time: 25 minutes
Nutritional Value (per serving):
Calories: 90, Protein: 3g, Fat: 7g, Carbs: 8g

Almond Butter Energy Bites

Ingredients:

- 1/2 cup almond butter
- 1/4 cup chia seeds
- 1/4 cup unsweetened shredded coconut
- 1 tablespoon honey
- 1/4 teaspoon cinnamon

Preparation:

1. Mix all ingredients in a bowl until well combined.
2. Roll into bite-sized balls and refrigerate for 30 minutes to set.

Time: 10 minutes prep + 30 minutes chill
Nutritional Value (per serving):
Calories: 120, Protein: 4g, Fat: 9g, Carbs: 6g

Cauliflower Tots

Ingredients:

- 2 cups grated cauliflower
- 1/4 cup almond flour
- 1 egg, lightly beaten
- 1/4 cup shredded cheese (optional)
- Salt and pepper to taste

Preparation:

1. Preheat oven to 375°F (190°C).
2. Mix all ingredients in a bowl and form into small tots.
3. Place on a baking sheet and bake for 20-25 minutes until golden brown.

Time: 25 minutes
Nutritional Value (per serving):
Calories: 80, Protein: 4g, Fat: 5g, Carbs: 5g

Baked Kale Chips

Ingredients:

- 1 bunch kale, stems removed and torn into pieces
- 1 tablespoon olive oil
- Salt to taste

Preparation:

1. Preheat oven to 300°F (150°C).
2. Toss kale with olive oil and salt.
3. Spread on a baking sheet and bake for 20 minutes, turning halfway, until crispy.

Time: 20 minutes
Nutritional Value (per serving):
Calories: 60, Protein: 2g, Fat: 4g, Carbs: 4g

Stuffed Mini Bell Peppers

Ingredients:

- 10 mini bell peppers, halved and seeds removed
- 1/2 cup cottage cheese or ricotta
- 1 tablespoon olive oil
- Salt and pepper to taste
- Fresh herbs for garnish (optional)

Preparation:

1. Stuff each mini bell pepper half with cottage cheese or ricotta.
2. Drizzle with olive oil and season with salt and pepper.
3. Garnish with fresh herbs if desired.

Time: 10 minutes
Nutritional Value (per serving):
Calories: 100, Protein: 6g, Fat: 5g, Carbs: 8g

Crispy Parmesan Cauliflower Bites

Ingredients:

- 1 small head cauliflower, cut into florets
- 1/4 cup grated Parmesan cheese
- 1 tablespoon olive oil
- Salt and pepper to taste

Preparation:

1. Preheat oven to 400°F (200°C).
2. Toss cauliflower florets with olive oil, Parmesan, salt, and pepper.
3. Spread on a baking sheet and roast for 20-25 minutes, until crispy and golden.

Time: 25 minutes
Nutritional Value (per serving):
Calories: 110, Protein: 5g, Fat: 7g, Carbs: 8g

These guilt-free snacks and sides are perfect for keeping you satisfied between meals or pairing with lunch and dinner, all while maintaining steady glucose levels and providing important nutrients.

Chapter 6: Refreshing Drinks and Smoothies

This chapter brings you 10 refreshing and healthy drinks and smoothies that keep you hydrated and energized while supporting balanced glucose levels. These drinks are designed to help you stay hydrated and satisfied without added sugars or processed ingredients.

Green Detox Smoothie

Ingredients:

- 1 cup spinach
- 1/2 cucumber
- 1/2 avocado
- 1 tablespoon chia seeds
- 1 cup unsweetened almond milk
- Juice of 1/2 lemon

Preparation:

1. Combine all ingredients in a blender and blend until smooth.
2. Serve immediately.

Time: 5 minutes
Nutritional Value (per serving):
Calories: 180, Protein: 4g, Fat: 12g, Carbs: 14g

Coconut Water and Berry Refresher

Ingredients:

- 1 cup coconut water
- 1/4 cup mixed berries (blueberries, strawberries, raspberries)
- Juice of 1 lime
- A few ice cubes

Preparation:

1. In a blender, mix the coconut water, berries, and lime juice.
2. Add ice cubes and blend until smooth.

Time: 5 minutes
Nutritional Value (per serving):
Calories: 70, Protein: 1g, Fat: 0g, Carbs: 15g

Mint and Cucumber Infused Water

Ingredients:

- 1/2 cucumber, sliced
- A handful of fresh mint leaves
- 1 liter water
- Ice cubes

Preparation:

1. In a large pitcher, add cucumber slices and mint leaves.
2. Fill with water and let it sit in the fridge for 1-2 hours.
3. Add ice cubes before serving.

Time: 5 minutes + infusion time
Nutritional Value: 0 calories, 0g protein, 0g fat, 0g carbs

Strawberry Basil Lemonade

Ingredients:

- 1/2 cup fresh strawberries
- 4 fresh basil leaves
- Juice of 2 lemons
- 2 cups water
- 1 tablespoon honey

Preparation:

1. Blend strawberries, basil, lemon juice, water, and honey until smooth.
2. Pour over ice and serve chilled.

Time: 10 minutes
Nutritional Value (per serving):
Calories: 80, Protein: 1g, Fat: 0g, Carbs: 21g

Turmeric Golden Milk

Ingredients:

- 1 cup unsweetened almond milk
- 1/2 teaspoon ground turmeric
- 1/4 teaspoon ground cinnamon
- 1/4 teaspoon ginger powder
- 1 teaspoon honey

Preparation:

1. Heat almond milk in a saucepan until warm.
2. Whisk in turmeric, cinnamon, ginger, and honey until combined.
3. Serve warm.

Time: 5 minutes
Nutritional Value (per serving):
Calories: 90, Protein: 1g, Fat: 3g, Carbs: 15g

Lemon Ginger Iced Tea

Ingredients:

- 4 cups water
- 1-inch piece fresh ginger, sliced
- Juice of 2 lemons
- Ice cubes
- 1 tablespoon honey (optional)

Preparation:

1. Boil water with ginger slices for 10 minutes.
2. Remove from heat, add lemon juice and honey (if using).
3. Let cool, then pour over ice and serve.

Time: 15 minutes
Nutritional Value (per serving):
Calories: 30, Protein: 0g, Fat: 0g, Carbs: 8g

Avocado Smoothie

Ingredients:

- 1/2 ripe avocado
- 1/2 banana
- 1 tablespoon chia seeds
- 1 cup unsweetened almond milk
- 1 teaspoon honey

Preparation:

1. Blend avocado, banana, chia seeds, almond milk, and honey until smooth.
2. Serve chilled.

Time: 5 minutes
Nutritional Value (per serving):
Calories: 240, Protein: 4g, Fat: 18g, Carbs: 20g

Cucumber Lemonade

Ingredients:

- 1 cucumber, peeled and sliced
- Juice of 2 lemons
- 2 cups water
- 1 tablespoon honey
- Ice cubes

Preparation:

1. Blend cucumber with lemon juice, water, and honey.
2. Pour over ice and serve chilled.

Time: 10 minutes
Nutritional Value (per serving):
Calories: 60, Protein: 1g, Fat: 0g, Carbs: 16g

Kale and Pineapple Smoothie

Ingredients:

- 1 cup chopped kale
- 1/2 cup fresh pineapple chunks
- 1/2 cup unsweetened almond milk
- 1 tablespoon chia seeds

Preparation:

1. Blend kale, pineapple, almond milk, and chia seeds until smooth.
2. Serve immediately.

Time: 5 minutes
Nutritional Value (per serving):
Calories: 120, Protein: 3g, Fat: 4g, Carbs: 19g

Herbal Iced Green Tea

Ingredients:

- 4 cups brewed green tea, chilled
- 1 tablespoon fresh mint leaves
- 1 tablespoon honey (optional)
- Ice cubes

Preparation:

1. Brew green tea and let it cool.
2. Add mint leaves and honey (if using).
3. Serve over ice.

Time: 10 minutes
Nutritional Value (per serving):
Calories: 20, Protein: 0g, Fat: 0g, Carbs: 6g

These refreshing drinks and smoothies are designed to be hydrating, energizing, and great for keeping your glucose levels stable while offering a variety of delicious flavors.

Chapter 7: Sweet Treats Without the Sugar

Desserts are often associated with indulgence, but with a few clever substitutions, you can enjoy sweet treats without the guilt or sugar spikes. This chapter offers 10 delicious dessert recipes that satisfy your sweet tooth while maintaining stable glucose levels, using natural sweeteners like **agave** or **honey** instead of refined sugar.

Coconut Flour Brownies

Ingredients:

- 1/2 cup coconut flour
- 1/4 cup unsweetened cocoa powder
- 1/3 cup honey
- 1/2 cup melted coconut oil
- 3 large eggs
- 1 teaspoon vanilla extract
- 1/4 teaspoon baking powder

Preparation:

1. Preheat oven to 350°F (175°C).
2. In a bowl, whisk together the coconut flour, cocoa powder, and baking powder.
3. Add honey, melted coconut oil, eggs, and vanilla extract. Mix until smooth.
4. Pour the batter into a greased baking dish and bake for 20-25 minutes.
5. Allow to cool before cutting into squares.

Time: 30 minutes
Nutritional Value (per serving):
Calories: 160, Protein: 4g, Fat: 11g, Carbs: 12g

Chia Pudding with Berries

Ingredients:

- 1/4 cup chia seeds
- 1 cup unsweetened almond milk
- 1 tablespoon honey
- 1/2 teaspoon vanilla extract
- 1/4 cup mixed berries

Preparation:

1. Combine chia seeds, almond milk, honey, and vanilla extract in a bowl.
2. Stir well and refrigerate overnight.
3. Serve topped with mixed berries.

Time: 10 minutes prep + overnight chill
Nutritional Value (per serving):
Calories: 180, Protein: 5g, Fat: 9g, Carbs: 21g

Almond Butter Chocolate Bites

Ingredients:

- 1/2 cup almond butter
- 1/4 cup unsweetened cocoa powder
- 1/4 cup honey
- 1/4 cup unsweetened shredded coconut

Preparation:

1. In a bowl, mix almond butter, cocoa powder, and honey until smooth.
2. Roll into bite-sized balls and coat with shredded coconut.
3. Refrigerate for 30 minutes before serving.

Time: 10 minutes prep + 30 minutes chill
Nutritional Value (per serving):
Calories: 130, Protein: 4g, Fat: 10g, Carbs: 9g

Avocado Chocolate Mousse

Ingredients:

- 2 ripe avocados
- 1/4 cup unsweetened cocoa powder
- 1/4 cup honey
- 1 teaspoon vanilla extract
- A pinch of sea salt

Preparation:

1. Blend the avocados, cocoa powder, honey, vanilla extract, and salt until smooth.
2. Serve chilled.

Time: 5 minutes
Nutritional Value (per serving):
Calories: 220, Protein: 3g, Fat: 15g, Carbs: 22g

Coconut Macaroons

Ingredients:

- 2 cups unsweetened shredded coconut
- 1/4 cup honey
- 2 large egg whites
- 1 teaspoon vanilla extract
- A pinch of salt

Preparation:

1. Preheat the oven to 325°F (160°C).
2. In a bowl, mix coconut, honey, egg whites, vanilla, and salt.
3. Drop spoonfuls of the mixture onto a parchment-lined baking sheet.
4. Bake for 15-18 minutes until golden brown.

Time: 20 minutes
Nutritional Value (per serving):
Calories: 110, Protein: 2g, Fat: 8g, Carbs: 8g

Baked Apples with Cinnamon

Ingredients:

- 4 apples, cored
- 2 tablespoons honey
- 1 teaspoon cinnamon
- 1/4 cup chopped walnuts

Preparation:

1. Preheat oven to 350°F (175°C).
2. Place the cored apples in a baking dish.
3. Drizzle honey inside the apples and sprinkle with cinnamon and chopped walnuts.
4. Bake for 25-30 minutes until tender.

Time: 30 minutes
Nutritional Value (per serving):
Calories: 160, Protein: 1g, Fat: 6g, Carbs: 28g

Lemon Coconut Energy Balls

Ingredients:

- 1 cup almond flour
- 1/4 cup unsweetened shredded coconut
- 1/4 cup honey
- Zest and juice of 1 lemon
- 1 tablespoon chia seeds

Preparation:

1. Mix all ingredients in a bowl until combined.
2. Roll the mixture into bite-sized balls and refrigerate for 30 minutes before serving.

Time: 10 minutes prep + 30 minutes chill
Nutritional Value (per serving):
Calories: 100, Protein: 2g, Fat: 6g, Carbs: 9g

Dark Chocolate and Almond Bark

Ingredients:

- 1/2 cup dark chocolate chips (at least 70% cocoa)
- 1/4 cup chopped almonds
- 1 tablespoon unsweetened shredded coconut

Preparation:

1. Melt the dark chocolate in a microwave-safe bowl in 30-second intervals, stirring in between.
2. Stir in chopped almonds and coconut.
3. Spread the mixture onto a parchment-lined baking sheet and refrigerate until firm.
4. Break into pieces before serving.

Time: 10 minutes prep + 20 minutes chill
Nutritional Value (per serving):
Calories: 150, Protein: 2g, Fat: 11g, Carbs: 12g

Berry Parfait with Greek Yogurt

Ingredients:

- 1/2 cup plain Greek yogurt
- 1/4 cup mixed berries
- 1 tablespoon chia seeds
- 1 teaspoon honey

Preparation:

1. Layer Greek yogurt with mixed berries and chia seeds.
2. Drizzle with honey before serving.

Time: 5 minutes
Nutritional Value (per serving):
Calories: 150, Protein: 8g, Fat: 4g, Carbs: 20g

Peanut Butter and Banana Ice Cream

Ingredients:

- 3 frozen bananas
- 2 tablespoons peanut butter
- 1 teaspoon vanilla extract

Preparation:

1. Blend the frozen bananas, peanut butter, and vanilla until smooth and creamy.
2. Serve immediately or freeze for an hour for a firmer texture.

Time: 5 minutes
Nutritional Value (per serving):
Calories: 180, Protein: 4g, Fat: 6g, Carbs: 29g

These sweet treats are perfect for satisfying your dessert cravings without refined sugars, offering healthier alternatives that are just as delicious while supporting balanced glucose levels.

Bonus: 28-Day Meal Plan for Balanced Glucose

This 28-day meal plan is designed to guide you through four weeks of balanced, nutritious meals that will help maintain steady glucose levels, support your energy needs, and keep you satisfied without refined carbs or sugars. Each day includes breakfast, lunch, dinner, and snacks, with a focus on whole foods, healthy fats, lean proteins, and fiber-rich vegetables.

Week 1	
	- **Breakfast**: Spinach and Mushroom Egg Scramble - **Lunch**: Chicken and Avocado Salad - **Dinner**: Lemon Garlic Baked Salmon with Broccoli - **Snack**: Cucumber and Hummus Bites
	- **Breakfast**: Chia Pudding with Berries - **Lunch**: Zucchini Noodles with Pesto and Shrimp - **Dinner**: Grilled Chicken with Roasted Brussels Sprouts - **Snack**: Avocado Deviled Eggs

	- **Breakfast**: Green Detox Smoothie - **Lunch**: Greek Quinoa Salad - **Dinner**: Stuffed Bell Peppers with Cauliflower Rice - **Snack**: Almond Butter Energy Bites
	- **Breakfast**: Coconut Flour Pancakes with Honey Drizzle - **Lunch**: Cobb Salad with Grilled Chicken - **Dinner**: Shrimp Stir-Fry with Vegetables - **Snack**: Zucchini Chips
	- **Breakfast**: Almond Flour Pancakes with Berries - **Lunch**: Baked Cod with Lemon and Asparagus - **Dinner**: Turkey Meatballs with Zucchini Noodles - **Snack**: Coconut Macaroons
	- **Breakfast**: Avocado and Cottage Cheese Bowl - **Lunch**: Grilled Steak with Roasted Brussels Sprouts - **Dinner**: Eggplant Lasagna - **Snack**: Crispy Roasted Chickpeas

	- **Breakfast**: Smoothie Bowl with Mixed Berries - **Lunch**: Spinach and Feta Omelet - **Dinner**: Chicken Lettuce Wraps - **Snack**: Baked Apples with Cinnamon
Week 2	
	- **Breakfast**: Chia Pudding with Berries - **Lunch**: Grilled Salmon with Asparagus - **Dinner**: Cauliflower Fried Rice with Chicken - **Snack**: Roasted Brussels Sprouts with Balsamic Glaze
	- **Breakfast**: Avocado Smoothie - **Lunch**: Spaghetti Squash with Marinara and Ground Beef - **Dinner**: Zucchini Noodles with Ground Turkey and Tomato Sauce - **Snack**: Stuffed Mini Bell Peppers
	- **Breakfast**: Egg Muffins with Spinach and Peppers - **Lunch**: Chicken and Avocado Salad - **Dinner**: Baked Cod with Lemon and Asparagus

	- **Snack**: Dark Chocolate and Almond Bark
	- **Breakfast**: Coconut Chia Seed Pudding - **Lunch**: Greek Quinoa Salad - **Dinner**: Grilled Chicken Caesar Salad - **Snack**: Lemon Coconut Energy Balls
	- **Breakfast**: Avocado and Cottage Cheese Bowl - **Lunch**: Stuffed Bell Peppers with Turkey and Spinach - **Dinner**: Grilled Steak with Roasted Brussels Sprouts - **Snack**: Peanut Butter and Banana Ice Cream
	- **Breakfast**: Quinoa Breakfast Bowl with Berries - **Lunch**: Shrimp Stir-Fry with Vegetables - **Dinner**: Eggplant Lasagna - **Snack**: Almond Butter Chocolate Bites
	- **Breakfast**: Spinach and Feta Omelet - **Lunch**: Zucchini Noodles with Pesto and Shrimp - **Dinner**: Turkey Meatballs with Zucchini Noodles - **Snack**: Cauliflower Tots

Week 3	
	- **Breakfast**: Almond Flour Pancakes with Honey
- **Lunch**: Grilled Chicken and Avocado Salad
- **Dinner**: Lemon Garlic Baked Salmon with Broccoli
- **Snack**: Almond Butter Energy Bites
	- **Breakfast**: Chia Pudding with Mixed Berries
- **Lunch**: Stuffed Bell Peppers with Ground Turkey
- **Dinner**: Baked Cod with Lemon and Asparagus
- **Snack**: Zucchini Chips
	- **Breakfast**: Green Detox Smoothie
- **Lunch**: Cobb Salad
- **Dinner**: Cauliflower Fried Rice with Chicken
- **Snack**: Roasted Brussels Sprouts with Balsamic Glaze
	- **Breakfast**: Scrambled Tofu with Spinach and Tomatoes
- **Lunch**: Grilled Salmon with Asparagus
- **Dinner**: Spaghetti Squash with Marinara and Ground Beef

	- **Snack**: Lemon Coconut Energy Balls
	- **Breakfast**: Avocado and Cottage Cheese Bowl - **Lunch**: Chicken Lettuce Wraps - **Dinner**: Shrimp Stir-Fry with Vegetables - **Snack**: Dark Chocolate and Almond Bark
	- **Breakfast**: Smoothie Bowl with Mixed Berries - **Lunch**: Greek Quinoa Salad - **Dinner**: Grilled Steak with Roasted Brussels Sprouts - **Snack**: Almond Butter Chocolate Bites
	- **Breakfast**: Spinach and Mushroom Scramble - **Lunch**: Chicken and Avocado Salad - **Dinner**: Turkey Meatballs with Zucchini Noodles - **Snack**: Coconut Macaroons
Week 4	
	- **Breakfast**: Avocado Smoothie - **Lunch**: Grilled Chicken Caesar Salad - **Dinner**: Baked Cod with Lemon and Asparagus

	• **Snack**: Peanut Butter and Banana Ice Cream
	• **Breakfast**: Coconut Chia Seed Pudding • **Lunch**: Stuffed Bell Peppers with Ground Beef • **Dinner**: Grilled Salmon with Asparagus • **Snack**: Zucchini Chips
	• **Breakfast**: Scrambled Tofu with Spinach and Tomatoes • **Lunch**: Cobb Salad • **Dinner**: Spaghetti Squash with Marinara and Ground Beef • **Snack**: Almond Butter Energy Bites
	• **Breakfast**: Green Detox Smoothie • **Lunch**: Chicken Lettuce Wraps • **Dinner**: Lemon Garlic Baked Salmon with Broccoli • **Snack**: Crispy Roasted Chickpeas
	• **Breakfast**: Avocado and Cottage Cheese Bowl • **Lunch**: Greek Quinoa Salad • **Dinner**: Eggplant Lasagna

	- **Snack**: Coconut Macaroons
	- **Breakfast**: Smoothie Bowl with Mixed Berries - **Lunch**: Grilled Steak with Roasted Brussels Sprouts - **Dinner**: Shrimp Stir-Fry with Vegetables - **Snack**: Dark Chocolate and Almond Bark
	- **Breakfast**: Almond Flour Pancakes with Berries - **Lunch**: Zucchini Noodles with Ground Turkey - **Dinner**: Baked Cod with Lemon and Asparagus - **Snack**: Lemon Coconut Energy Balls

This 28-day meal plan ensures a variety of flavors, textures, and nutrient-rich meals that promote steady glucose levels and balanced energy. Each week offers different breakfast, lunch, dinner, and snack options to keep you feeling full and satisfied.

Bonus: 28-Day Meal Plan Shopping List

To help you stay organized as you prepare for your 28-day meal plan, here's a comprehensive shopping list. I've grouped ingredients by category to make it easier for you to shop at your local grocery store. This list covers everything you'll need for the breakfasts, lunches, dinners, and snacks outlined in the meal plan from Chapter 8.

Produce	

	- **Greens & Herbs**:
	  - Spinach (fresh or frozen)
	  - Kale
	  - Mixed greens
	  - Romaine lettuce
	  - Fresh basil
	  - Fresh parsley
	  - Fresh cilantro
	  - Fresh mint

	- **Vegetables**: - Zucchinis (for noodles and chips)

	<ul><li>Bell peppers (variety of colors)</li><li>Broccoli</li><li>Cauliflower (whole or pre-riced)</li><li>Brussels sprouts</li><li>Asparagus</li><li>Cucumber</li><li>Tomatoes (cherry and regular)</li><li>Eggplant</li><li>Carrots</li><li>Mini bell peppers</li><li>Avocados (multiple)</li></ul>
	- **Fruits**:<ul><li>Mixed berries (strawberries, raspberries, blueberries)</li><li>Lemons</li><li>Limes</li><li>Apples</li><li>Bananas</li><li>Pineapple (fresh or frozen)</li><li>Coconut (unsweetened shredded)</li></ul>
Proteins	

- **Meat & Poultry**:
    - Chicken breasts (boneless, skinless)
    - Ground chicken
    - Ground turkey
    - Ground beef
    - Steak (sirloin or ribeye)
    - Bacon

- **Seafood**:
    - Salmon fillets
    - Cod fillets
    - Shrimp (peeled and deveined)
    - Smoked salmon

- **Eggs & Dairy**:
    - Large eggs
    - Cottage cheese
    - Ricotta cheese
    - Feta cheese
    - Mozzarella cheese
    - Parmesan cheese
    - Cheddar cheese

	○ Greek yogurt (plain, unsweetened)
Pantry Staples	

	- **Nuts, Seeds, & Grains**:
	    ○ Almonds (whole and sliced)
	    ○ Chia seeds
	    ○ Almond flour
	    ○ Coconut flour
	    ○ Quinoa

	- **Oils, Vinegars, & Condiments**:
	    ○ Olive oil
	    ○ Coconut oil
	    ○ Balsamic vinegar
	    ○ Apple cider vinegar
	    ○ Soy sauce (or tamari for gluten-free)
	    ○ Dijon mustard
	    ○ Peanut butter (unsweetened)
	    ○ Almond butter

	- **Canned Goods**:
	    ○ Chickpeas (canned)
	    ○ Tomato sauce (low-sugar)
	    ○ Coconut milk (unsweetened)
	    ○ Tuna (canned, in water)
	    ○ Chicken broth or vegetable broth (low-sodium)
	    ○ Hummus (optional, or make your own)

	- **Spices & Seasonings**:
	    ○ Salt
	    ○ Pepper
	    ○ Smoked paprika
	    ○ Ground turmeric
	    ○ Ground cinnamon
	    ○ Ground ginger
	    ○ Garlic powder
	    ○ Italian seasoning
	    ○ Oregano
	    ○ Cumin

Natural Sweeteners	- Honey - Agave syrup

	- Dark chocolate (at least 70% cocoa)
Frozen Items	- Frozen mixed berries (for smoothies) - Frozen spinach (for omelets, smoothies, etc.) - Frozen cauliflower rice (optional, or make your own)
Beverages	- Coconut water - Almond milk (unsweetened) - Green tea - Herbal tea
Miscellaneous	- Low-carb or keto-friendly bread (for avocado toast) - Zucchini spiralizer (if making your own zucchini noodles) - Food storage containers (for meal prep and leftovers)

This shopping list will ensure you have everything you need to follow the 28-day meal plan with ease. By stocking up on these essentials, you can stay organized and keep your meals on track for the next four weeks. Happy cooking!

Bonus: Tips for Long-Term Success

Congratulations on making it through the 28-day meal plan and embracing a new way of eating that prioritizes stable glucose levels and overall well-being. In this final chapter, I want to share some helpful strategies and tips to ensure your long-term success in maintaining a balanced diet that supports your health goals. Remember, this journey isn't just about short-term changes but developing habits that you can sustain for life.

Meal Prepping and Planning Ahead

One of the best ways to stay on track is by dedicating time each week to meal prepping and planning. Meal prepping ensures that you always have healthy, balanced meals on hand, which reduces the temptation to reach for less nutritious options when you're busy or tired.

- **Set Aside Time**: Schedule one or two days a week for meal prep. You can batch-cook proteins like chicken, roast vegetables, and prepare grains like quinoa to have ready for quick meals.
- **Pre-Pack Snacks**: Having pre-portioned, healthy snacks like roasted chickpeas, hummus with veggies, or energy bites will help you avoid grabbing processed or sugary snacks.
- **Store Efficiently**: Use airtight containers to store your prepped meals in the fridge or freezer to maintain freshness throughout the week.

Understanding Portion Sizes

Portion control is key when following a balanced eating plan. Even healthy foods can lead to overeating if portion sizes are too large, which can disrupt your glucose levels. Use tools like measuring cups or a food scale to get a better understanding of what a balanced portion looks like, especially for carbohydrate-dense foods like quinoa or sweet potatoes.

- **Balance Your Plate**: Fill half of your plate with vegetables, a quarter with protein, and a quarter with healthy fats or slow-digesting carbs.
- **Mindful Eating**: Eat slowly, savor each bite, and pay attention to your body's hunger cues to avoid overeating.

Healthy Substitutions for Common Cravings

Cravings for sweet or salty foods are normal, but you can satisfy them without compromising your balanced eating habits. Learn to make simple swaps that help you stay on track while still enjoying your favorite flavors.

- **Craving Sweets?** Opt for snacks like chia seed pudding with berries, almond butter chocolate bites, or baked apples with cinnamon instead of refined sugar-laden desserts.
- **Craving Crunchy Snacks?** Try roasted chickpeas, baked kale chips, or zucchini chips as alternatives to processed, salty snacks like chips or crackers.

Staying Hydrated

Hydration plays an important role in maintaining energy levels and supporting healthy digestion. Often, when we feel hungry, we're actually thirsty. Make sure to drink plenty of water throughout the day, and incorporate hydrating beverages like herbal teas and infused water.

- **Start Your Day with Water**: Drink a glass of water first thing in the morning to jumpstart your hydration.
- **Infuse for Flavor**: Add lemon, cucumber, mint, or berries to your water to make it more flavorful and enjoyable to drink.

Dealing with Social Situations

Dining out or attending social gatherings can sometimes be challenging when you're following a specific eating plan. However, with a bit of preparation, you can stay on track without feeling deprived.

- **Check Menus in Advance**: Many restaurants post their menus online, so take a few minutes to look up options that align with your eating plan before you go.
- **Don't Be Afraid to Ask for Modifications**: Request substitutions like extra vegetables instead of bread or ask for sauces and dressings on the side.
- **Bring a Healthy Dish**: If you're attending a potluck or gathering, bring a dish like a salad, roasted vegetables, or energy bites to ensure there's a healthy option available.

Navigating Emotional Eating

Emotional eating is a common challenge that can derail healthy eating habits. Recognize the difference between emotional hunger and physical hunger, and learn strategies to cope with emotional triggers without turning to food for comfort.

- **Mindful Eating**: Practice mindfulness by checking in with yourself before reaching for food. Ask yourself if you're truly hungry or if you're eating due to stress, boredom, or other emotions.
- **Find Alternatives**: When emotional hunger strikes, try alternatives like going for a walk, journaling, or calling a friend for support.

Maintaining Consistency

Consistency is the key to long-term success. While it's okay to enjoy occasional indulgences, maintaining a consistent eating pattern will help you achieve and sustain your health goals.

- **Create Routine**: Stick to regular meal times and focus on balanced, nutrient-dense meals. This will help regulate your energy levels and prevent unnecessary snacking.
- **Don't Aim for Perfection**: It's important to be flexible and allow yourself some freedom. One off-plan meal won't undo your progress. Get back on track at the next meal and focus on long-term consistency rather than short-term perfection.

Celebrating Progress and Staying Motivated

Change is gradual, and it's important to celebrate the small victories along the way. Whether it's feeling more energized, fitting into clothes more comfortably, or simply feeling good about your food choices, these are all milestones worth celebrating.

- **Set Realistic Goals**: Focus on achievable goals like trying new recipes, meal prepping consistently, or drinking more water.
- **Track Your Success**: Keep a journal of your progress, including how you feel physically and mentally as you adopt healthier eating habits.

This chapter is designed to give you the tools and knowledge needed to maintain your healthy eating habits beyond the 28-day meal plan. By focusing on consistency, balance, and mindful eating, you'll set yourself up for long-term success and enjoy all the benefits of steady glucose levels, improved energy, and overall well-being. Happy cooking, and cheers to a healthier, more balanced life!

Conclusion

Thank you for taking the time to explore this *Glucose Revolution Cookbook* with me. Throughout this journey, we've covered a wide range of delicious, nutritious recipes designed to support balanced glucose levels and provide sustained energy without the need for refined sugars or carbs. Whether you're just beginning your health journey or are a seasoned pro, this book has equipped you with practical tools and tasty recipes that nourish your body while keeping your blood sugar stable.

The ultimate goal of this book has been to show you that eating for glucose balance doesn't mean sacrificing flavor or enjoyment. From energizing breakfasts to hearty lunches, light dinners, and satisfying snacks, these recipes were crafted to be flexible, simple, and adaptable to your lifestyle. By embracing wholesome ingredients like healthy fats, lean proteins, fiber-rich vegetables, and natural sweeteners, you can create meals that not only taste great but also support long-term health and well-being.

As you move forward, I encourage you to continue experimenting with the recipes, adjusting them to your personal preferences, and applying the tips shared throughout the book. Remember, this isn't just about following a strict plan—it's about building sustainable habits that align with your goals and allow you to enjoy food in a way that makes you feel your best.

The power of stable glucose levels is transformative, impacting your energy, mood, focus, and overall health. I hope the knowledge, recipes, and meal plans shared here empower you to take control of your health and enjoy every step of the process.

Here's to your continued success, vibrant health, and many more delicious meals ahead!